M000317896

The Truth in Dissonance

The Truth in Dissonance

Poems by

Jean L. Kreiling

For Faye –
Thanks for your support!

Jean L Kreiling

Kelsay Books

© 2014 Jean L. Kreiling. All rights reserved. This material may not be reproduced in any form, published, reprinted, recorded, performed, broadcast, rewritten or redistributed without the explicit permission of Jean L. Kreiling. All such actions are strictly prohibited by law.

Cover Art: *cacophony,* acrylic on panel
        by Regina Valluzzi
        http://www.Nerdlypainter.com

ISBN 13: 978-0692250594

Kelsay Books
White Violet Press
www.kelsaybooks.com

For Ma and Dad

Acknowledgements

I extend heartfelt thanks to the editors of the journals and anthologies in which many of these poems first appeared, some in slightly different versions or under different titles:

14 by 14: "At Last," "August," "The Lilac," "Livingston
    Taylor Live," "Piano Duo"
American Arts Quarterly: "To the Ocean in Summer"
Angle: "Boston Common at Twilight," "In Autumn's
    Rust," "Paul and Ringo," "Pantoum for a
    Disappearing Pair," "Remnant"
Antiphon: "Ovillejo for the Librarian"
Autumn Sky Poetry: "Deck of a Beam Trawler,
    Gloucester," "Tide and Terrain"
Birchsong: Poetry Centered in Vermont (Danby, VT:
    Blueline Press, 2012): "To a Hummingbird"
Bloodroot Literary Magazine: "The Cobbler"
The Cannon's Mouth: "Winter Boats"
Dogwood: "Sometime After the Golden Anniversary"
The Edge City Review: "Pas de Deux"
Ekphrasis: "Gypsy Rondo," "Listening to Dido's Lament"
The Evansville Review: "Four Movements for Siblings,"
    "The Pianist's Prayer," "Subtext for Sam"
The Flea: "Perchance to Run"
The Ghazal Page: "A No-Garden Ghazal"
Literary Bohemian: "Newport Mansions"
Lucid Rhythms: "A Daughter Prepares to Leave for
    College," "Rondeau for Father McKenzie,"
    "Rondeau for Miss Rigby"
The Lyric: "Love and Shoes" "Porch Lights"
Measure: "The Caregiver-Wife," "Early Rehearsal,"
    "Little Girl Lost," "The New Homeowner"

Mezzo Cammin: "Another Plaster Idol Smashed to Bits,
          "At the Movies," "Ceiling Fans," "Playlist of the
          Woeful Middle-Aged Man"
New Walk: "Mute Migrants"
Off the Coast: "No Escape"
Pennsylvania Review: "In the Alto Section"
Shot Glass Journal: "Winter Confrontations"
SLANT: "The Philandering Professor Gets His
          Comeuppance"
Snakeskin: "Senryū for Uncle Sid"
String Poet: "At My Mother-in-Law's House," "At
          Symphony Hall"
Think Journal: "Gustav Mahler's *Kindertotenlieder*"
Tilt-a-Whirl: "Retirement Community Fauna"
Tower Journal: "December," "January"

Contents

II. The Truth in Dissonance

III. A Year in New England

IV. Bliss

I

Life's Crooked Lines

Narrative Arc

"Shape was the novelist's lie." —Sarah Blake, *The Postmistress*

Shape is the novelist's lie,
and plan is the minister's fib.
They sell us what we want to buy,
their persuasion poetic or glib.

As a story or sermon proceeds,
we succumb to a narrative spell:
the arcs of romances and creeds
trace the contours of heaven and hell.

Conditioned to trust the designs
that both fiction and worship require,
we're confounded by life's crooked lines
and by truth, as amorphous as fire.

The Cobbler

Of course you're grateful for the rough-cut scraps
of happiness from which you've learned to cobble
a life, but sometimes all that cobbling saps
your zest for living it. And then you hobble,
as others all around you seem to glide
through lives designed by Prada. You maintain
a decent pace, a serviceable stride
fueled by denial, and you don't complain;
in fact, when others find their spike heels mired
in excess, you lend your support, sincerely—
while closeting the signs of just how tired
and bruised you are yourself. Sometimes you nearly
succeed in fending off your foot-sore blues—
but still, you wish that you had better shoes.

At My Mother-in-Law's House

The bookshelves in her parlor, so well-stocked
they sagged, supplied excuses to suspend
strained chatter. I read some Thoreau, she rocked
and sniffed, we waited for the day to end.
Dinner was awkward. Though she'd done her best—
the roast well-seasoned, pie crust neatly crimped—
I felt too keenly that she'd never blessed
the tie that bound us; conversation limped.
But as I left, she gave me the Thoreau,
insisting gruffly that I keep the book.
Just how much that gift must have meant to her
escaped me then, but now, of course, I know:
it's clear each time I open it and look
at her dead husband's fading signature.

Ovillejo for the Librarian

"Four weeks," she says, as she hands back
a stack
of books checked out to me—bound herds
of words
I'll milk all month. It's life she lends,
and friends
to share it with. Though she pretends
they're only pages, I can sense
she knows she gives me sustenance:
a stack of words and friends.

Tanka for a Trucker

Brawny tires, rolling
with apparent ease, bear tons.
What weight do you bear
with your cobra-inked biceps
or behind your mile-glazed eyes?

Deck of a Beam Trawler, Gloucester

(after the painting by Edward Hopper)

He saw the art of work, despite the lack
of workers: the expectant energy
aboard the unmanned deck, the sinewy
preparedness of heavy ropes left slack,
the muscle of the mast. Where rusty black
abuts the dullish red of industry,
we know men labored, though we cannot see
their forms or faces or what they brought back.
They likely sailed before this sky turned blue,
before sunlit perspective clarified
the architecture of their work; they would
have felt their way through chores. The trawler's crew—
unlike the painter—didn't need a tide
of light to show them work they understood.

Little Girl Lost

(Long Beach, Rockport, MA)

"The family is clinging to the hope [she] is . . . with a stranger."
—*CBSBoston.com,* May 11, 2012.

Her dark-eyed parents have to look away;
they neither watch nor hear the wind-whipped water
that roars their anguish. Resolutely, they
imagine other torments for their daughter:
they hope that she's been kidnapped. They've been praying
that someone harmless, maybe someone lonely,
and charmed by their girl, longed to watch her playing
and giggling on some other beach. If only
some childless woman, kindly but misguided,
were even now retying a small shoe
or combing that fine hair . . . yes, they've decided:
they choose abduction. I think I would, too;
the only other possibility
is that their girl was taken by the sea.

And if their girl was taken by the sea—
the only culprit one wet surge that bore
their girl away, that bears the blame—no plea
for mercy would return her to this shore;
she never would be brought back to them whole,
or slightly broken, ready to be mended
with loving stitches. No, somebody stole
their girl. But no harm could have been intended
for her, who loves her sister and string cheese,
who grins at goldfish and who would have smiled
at some new friend. Of all the fantasies
that parents harbor for a growing child,
theirs has to be among the more bizarre:
the dream that she got into someone's car.

The dream that she got into someone's car
consoles them, even if that someone drove
too fast and even if their girl is far
from home, from their familiar sandy cove.
Their beach had seemed a safer spot than most—
the boardwalk offering a sturdy path,
the rocks along this stretch of scruffy coast
a barrier to waves of ocean wrath.
But such protection hadn't been enough.
Her mother blames herself: for just one second,
she'd turned to fetch a ball. The surf was rough,
too loud for her to hear if someone beckoned,
then took their girl. She turned and saw blank space
where she'd just seen her toddler's laughing face.

Where she'd just seen her toddler's laughing face,
the empty air now made her stomach lurch.
She shouted, ran, got help, and in a race
with time, authorities joined in the search.
Days later, those officials called a halt
to their investigation; they'd concluded
that only ocean currents were at fault—
a call the parents can't leave undisputed.
Those efforts must go on; yes, every man
and woman must keep looking, analyzing
each tiny clue, they must do all they can—
but some of us can't keep from scrutinizing
the realm where one small girl would have no chance:
that foaming, wild, unstoppable expanse.

That foaming, wild, unstoppable expanse
is calm now, at the harbor where we've met
with candles that sustain our hopeful trance
and light our promise that we won't forget.
This vigil joins us all in bright resistance
to loss; a beacon shines in every hand,
the girl's way back as clear as the persistence
of salty tides that lick the thirsty land.
Although we know that elsewhere it still seethes,
this evening's tranquil sea appears to bless
our confidence that one small girl still breathes
and will come home. All dimpled eagerness,
she'd watch the whitecaps where the seagulls play;
her dark-eyed parents have to look away.

A No-Garden Ghazal

No pinks, no pansies, no petunias—not this spring.
I only stare at my unplanted plot this spring.

Year after year, I've coaxed the colors from the dirt;
my neighbors must be thinking I forgot this spring.

They don't know that unfolding leaves would close my throat,
that sunlight only makes my tears burn hot this spring.

The brazen health of bursting buds would nauseate
a stomach that's already in a knot this spring.

I can't bear kneeling down to dig and weed and prune;
I've knelt—in earnest, but in vain—a lot this spring.

Where loss has put down roots, no stems will rise;
a crop of stones would have a better shot this spring.

Why nurture red and violet ephemera?
Why watch them fall to drought and pests and rot this spring?

I'll watch the neighbors' marigolds and daisies thrive,
their distant vigor all the hope I've got this spring.

I'll know that grief has eased if I can plant a few
naïvely dazzling dahlias in a pot this spring.

To a Hummingbird

Oh, blur of bird!

Please teach me how to hover weightlessly,
exquisitely escaping gravity,
and how to reach the speed of shimmering
and shapelessness, so that my movements sing.

Please show me how to flutter in reverse—
disturbing destiny, foiling a curse—
and how to find in bugs the nourishment
that nectar lacks. Teach me to be content

with pleasures blurred.

Early Rehearsal

At six a.m. I watch the sky rehearse
the day to come, as rose-rimmed shadows find
within the sun's old script a universe
brand-new and intricate, to light inclined—
but darkness lingers in the wings. What burns
in sun-struck pink is subject to the whim
of winds and fronts; as terra firma turns,
it spins a tale of futures that may dim.
Each second brings another set design,
another spotlit scene beyond prediction;
the brightening horizon learns its line
as dawn outdoes the facile plots of fiction.
Upstaged again, night exits, and I see
the sky emote with possibility.

.

At the Movies

"He is a moviegoer, though of course he does not go to movies."
—Walker Percy, *The Moviegoer*

He watches moving pictures in his mind,
while granting real life minimal attention;
he much prefers the scenes that he's designed.

He sleepwalks through his day—the office grind,
the past-due bills, the marital contention—
while watching moving pictures in his mind.

In his director's cut, the deal is signed,
the girl is hot, the car is fast—no mention
of trouble. In the scenes that he's designed,

he's young, he's rich, and he can always find
his keys. The screenplay sizzles with invention,
and so he watches pictures in his mind.

Engaged with an imagined cast, he's blind
to co-stars in the flesh, who might bring tension
or tedium to scenes that he's designed.

Nobody watches with him. Disinclined
to live in the quotidian dimension,
he moves alone through pictures in his mind,
and much prefers the scenes that he's designed.

The New Homeowner

1. *At the Closing*

In looping runes along straight lines,
he signs,
a gambler in a legal game,
his name
the ante—paid in cursive, then
again
on one more page—no, two—no, ten—
until all sense has left the letters.
With faith as blind as any bettor's,
he signs his name again.

2. *Keys*

He unabashedly enjoys
the noise:
the tinny, jingling melodies
of keys
that unlock rooms and lives unknown.
His own
collection has a rattling tone,
just deepened by a new addition—
his house key.   He hears pride, ambition:
the noise of keys—his own.

3. *Home Ownership*

He'll scrub and caulk the shower stall;
it's all
mildewed and cracked. He's shelling out
about
a month's pay for new floors downstairs;
repairs

to deck and roof are next. He swears
at doors that stick and taps that drip;
he understands home ownership:
it's all about repairs.

Porch Lights

Some people leave their porch lights on all night—
a signal, warmer than a welcome mat,
to curfew-breaking sons, or guests who might
come after all, or a returning cat.
Some leave their lights on to repel the ghostly
potential of the dark; abused or fretful,
they mean to warn intruders off. But mostly,
bright porches mark the homes of the forgetful:
the dad gets in late, focused on his itch
for scotch; the mom's caught up in Danielle Steel;
the daughter, texting, walks right past the switch—
and none of them suspects the curb appeal
a porch light adds. A glowing semaphore,
it hints that kindness lives behind their door.

Mailbox Montage

A pair of painted golfers, dressed in plaid,
lives on the mailbox fronting number forty;
they grip their clubs, perpetually glad
to play a round, meticulously sporty.

At number forty-five, across the street,
a plain white mailbox murmurs its address
in small blue numbers. Cheerful but discreet,
it hints at both refinement and success.

A gardener must live at forty-eight:
fresh pansies fill a planter by the box.
Their smiling purple faces mitigate
the stress of bills and nasty mail-borne shocks.

The green mailbox at number fifty-one
respectfully blends in with shrubs and vines;
its red flag flashes in the morning sun,
as red wings ornament the nearby pines.

At fifty-four, where crabgrass plagues the lawn,
a rusty mailbox leans alarmingly.
Its mouth agape, flag dangling (nearly gone),
it hints at need—perhaps catastrophe.

But just as covers don't define their books,
a mailbox may not perfectly reflect
the lives of those in charge of how it looks.
Who knows what might explain mailbox neglect?

The patchy yard at fifty-four might mean
that kids and parents have been playing tag
instead of keeping grass well-trimmed and green
and making sure the mailbox doesn't sag.

They probably should make time for a chore
or two—prop up the mailbox, skip one game—
but if the neighborhood is keeping score,
this family might win envy more than blame.

And rumor has it that the golfing folks
at number forty were just separated;
they're counting grievances instead of strokes,
their lives a mess, though smartly decorated.

Ceiling Fans

I

Fan blades, discreet as ladies wearing crisp
white gloves, reorganize the breathless heat
with prim, persistent gestures and a lisp
of whispered diligence doomed to defeat.
The potted palm below declines to bend
or sway—each long green finger still as stone—
as tiny tremors in the air descend
just inches from the path the blades have flown.
In woven wicker close beside the palm,
a woman sits and reads; she turns a page
and then looks up, inquisitive but calm,
with all the straight-spined patience of a sage.
She almost envies the insensate blade:
it doesn't recognize its own charade.

II

At three a.m., he heard the ceiling fan—
its rhythm regular, uncomplicated,
and scolding. He was not much of a man,
or so the hissing blades insinuated.
He barely saw them in the thin light seeping
through heavy drapes, but their persistent thrum
kept worries whirling and kept him from sleeping,
as if they murmured of what he'd become.
The churning susurration chanted *less!*—
you're jobless, wifeless, almost homeless!—and
your fault, your fault, your fault! His wakefulness
gave shape and weight to airy reprimand.
His dreams would skew the scolding into rasping,
relentless threats, and he would wake up gasping.

III

She woke up in the dark, and thought of wailing—
her crib was lonely, blanketless, and barred—
but first she looked toward the upper railing
where soft arms sometimes stretched over the hard
oak barrier to lift her into all
she needed: warmth, and singing, and the feeling
that she belonged, that she would never fall,
that milk was near. But something on the ceiling
distracted her. A movement caught her eye:
a steady spinning, shadows quickly turning
and shushing in a grayish game, too high
for her to join in, but she watched, soon learning
its placid patience—and her wide-eyed trance
spun into sleep beneath its faithful dance.

No Escape

He guns the engine, just to hear it roar:
a barrel-chested, thunderous last word.
He'd slammed out of the house, but that screen door
had barely slapped. Now, sure that he's been heard,
he takes off, elbow out the window, aping
his father's driving posture, unaware
that so much of what he thinks he's escaping
has hitched a ride, has filled his tires with air,
has fueled the bellowing of his V-8,
and now glares in his windshield. Peering past
blind rage, he sees enough to navigate
around the potholes, and goes nowhere fast.
His left forearm, like that of his old man,
will always wear a slightly darker tan.

A Daughter Prepares to Leave for College

She's packing boxes, loading up our car,
and emptying our nest—the old cliché—
she's ready, and she's braver than we are.

We've raised her well, she's been our shining star,
but we admit that our mood's dark today,
as she packs boxes and loads up our car.

Four hours down the road is much too far;
we tell her we'll be just a call away,
and hope she's really braver than we are.

She's taking stuffed bears, high heels, her guitar,
and half our hearts. Though we wish she could stay,
we help her pack a box and load the car.

She'll open new doors. Will she leave ajar
the door through which we've watched her grow and play?
She's ready to move on. How brave we are

to nod and smile as pride and sorrow spar:
we wish her well, we wish for some delay.
She's loaded one last box into our car;
she's ready, and she's braver than we are.

The Philandering Professor Gets His
Comeuppance

It was a foolish posture—but the whole
idea had been preposterous—to think
he'd give his young T.A. a lift, cajole
her into sharing more than just a drink,
impress her with his intellect, and then . . .
But now they'd reached the parking lot, to find
he couldn't find his car. Yes, once again
a useful fact had slipped his aging mind.
And so he stood at lot's edge, with his hand
held high as if to claim he knew the answer;
he pressed "unlock" on his remote and strained
to hear his Honda's mocking hoots. Unmanned
at just the moment he'd meant to romance her,
he knew that she must think him scatter-brained.

Or maybe she would think his addle-brained
behavior masked some deeper genius. Where
the dickens had he parked?   His prospects waned
along with macho pretense. Hand in air,
he furiously jabbed "unlock," but heard
no answering "beep-beep." Should he just roam
the lot and search? He knew he looked absurd.
Hell, at this point he'd rather just go home.
That's when he saw a pair of headlights swing
around the corner, saw the driver steer
right towards him, and—oh, damn, this wasn't cool—
his wife behind the wheel, maneuvering
his own old Honda. It was all so clear:
more than his posture marked him as a fool.

Senryū for Uncle Sid

Twilight. His Old Spice
aura has long since deferred
to scotch and Pall Malls.

His bare skull and limp
jowls are trumped by the feline
glitter in his eyes.

Planted in his chair,
he clears his throat and glowers
at his wheezing friend.

While Frank deals the cards
and grimly sips his decaf,
Sid snorts and mutters.

He squints at his hand.
Inhales, imbibes. Decides to
let Frank win this one.

Retirement Community Fauna

En route to its well-tended habitat,
a golf cart glides, its tiny engine purring.
With all the smug discretion of a cat
en route to its well-tended habitat,
it carries a feline aristocrat
who does not purr, but grins. He likes the whirring
of wheels en route toward his habitat.
The golf cart glides, its tiny engine purring.

Bridge tables buzz like hives of bumblebees,
the bidding honeyed by fast-flying rumor.
Marie has gout, Joan's getting two new knees,
or so they buzz. Like hives of bumblebees,
they're busy: "Two hearts." "Pass the peanuts, please."
They laugh; the sting of age requires humor
and hives of friends. They buzz like bumblebees,
their bidding honeyed by fast-flying rumor.

Liz never squawks about her aching wing;
her "golden" silence signifies endurance.
She coos about the grandkids visiting,
but never squawks about her aching wing.
Because the doctor couldn't do a thing,
and then some bird-brain screwed up her insurance,
she never squawks about her aching wing.
Her "golden"' silence signifies endurance.

A beast of burden once, George isn't sure
how best to prowl through permanent vacation.
Go fishing? Read? Take that wine-tasting tour?
A beast of burden once, he isn't sure.
He's learned to sleep late—sometimes doesn't stir
'til eight—but isn't fit for hibernation.
A beast of burden once, he's just not sure
how best to prowl through permanent vacation.

Exotic species visit every year,
each creature tethered to a high-tech toy—
young cubs with smart phones, pups with video gear—
so tall, and more exotic every year.
Although grandparents call the odd ducks "dear,"
bewilderment accompanies their joy
when alien species visit every year,
each creature tethered to a high-tech toy.

Swans mate for life; the lucky ones retire
to pretty ponds and float for years together.
For buoyancy, to cuddle and conspire,
swans mate for life. The lucky ones retire
and fluff each other's feathers. We admire
their loyalty, their grace, their pond's fine weather—
and we too hope to mate for life, retire
to pretty ponds, and float for years together.

My Father's Hands

Iron-sinewed hands
that once fixed, soothed, and scolded
now clutch at the bones
of reason, but grasp only
the fleshy grief in my wrists.

He studies his watch,
desperate to know this hour;
I start to explain
the hands and the numbers, but
he can't see through panic's fog.

A caregiver clips
his nails, washes his sparse hair,
coaxes him to eat
his eggs. When her shift ends, he
reaches out to shake her hand.

The Caregiver-Wife

She's under "stress"—a buzzword that's proclaimed
as if it's news—a much too tidy sound
for this life of well-woven plans unwound,
these golden years turned brass, this marriage maimed
by his disease and her too patly named
response: her pity, love, and anger bound
to the mast of a grand ship run aground
and wrecked, its rudder smashed, its compass lamed.
They call it stress—one syllable, one vowel,
a neat economy of consonants—
but she deals with the dreadful daily mess
of his disoriented brain and bowel;
she wades through waves of heartbreak so immense
that she may drown in seas of so-called stress.

Perchance to Run

You dream of running, feel your legs extending
beyond a sprinter's reach into ballet,
elastic knees and elbows blithely bending,
uncompromised by decades of decay.
You barely touch the earth—each stride propelled
by just a moment's contact with the ground,
the government of gravity now felled
as fantasy inflates each buoyant bound.
Immune from waking weariness, endowed
with lungs of limitless capacity,
You fly through sleep's accommodating cloud,
and never doubt the dream's veracity.
Awakened by the clock's alarming bleat,
you hardly recognize your own clay feet.

South Carolina Morning

(after the painting by Edward Hopper)

Well, I know I look fine in this red dress,
but no one in this swamp has any taste.
I'm so tired of pale grass and emptiness,
this too-big sky, this heat as thick as paste.
I only came because Belinda Ann
laid on the guilt: "We haven't seen you, Kitty,
for ages now." Three years ago I ran
away from this backwater to the city—
but I have missed my Daddy, so I'm here.
Now Mama mutters that my hat is fussy,
the neckline of my dress too low; it's clear
she thinks high heels make me some kind of hussy.
If she unpursed her lips, I think she'd hiss.
And I got myself all dolled up for this?

Yes, I got myself all dolled up for this
big party—Daddy's turning sixty-eight.
He's dozing, probably content to miss
the half-baked revelry. He'll celebrate
in bourbon's blurred embrace; he'll hardly see
Aunt Kate's dog shedding in his Morris chair,
Belinda Ann's dim-witted husband Lee,
their bratty kids, my brother Al's long hair.
I know my Daddy; I know how he dealt
with years of Mama's miserly affection;
I'm sure he just tossed back an extra belt
the day of my undaughterly defection.
This party reeks of all he can't abide,
so he indulges in slow suicide.

While he indulges in slow suicide,
I save myself, abandoning the heat
of family friction, venturing outside,
but finding no relief in my retreat.
I breathe in something cottony and thick,
the same damp flannel that weighs on my skin.
Both air and history make me feel sick;
I crave some other atmosphere and kin.
Belinda Ann, dear sister, grinned with spite
when Mama blanched at my V-neck; Aunt Kate
half-sputtered that my dress looked mighty tight;
while Al shot me a leer of need and hate.
I know that I should go back in there soon.
How will I tolerate the afternoon?

How will I tolerate an afternoon
of righteousness and rumors and regret?
Hell, will I last the morning? That buffoon
Belinda Ann got married to has set
his mind on getting Daddy's ear; he's yelling
some birthday toast, and then he yells at me
to come back in. Well, he sure isn't telling
me what to do. I try to smell the sea;
it isn't far, but you would never know
that wind and water move around nearby.
It's all so still and stagnant here, below
the heavy oilcloth of this dense blue sky.
Unchecked, this sun would ruin my complexion;
this hat's for style, but also for protection.

My hat's for style, but also for protection
against the unrelenting glare that burns
and wrinkles you. I have quite a collection
of hats and shoes; in town, my wardrobe earns
me lots of compliments. I guess I should
have known that back here I'd look out of place;
three years ago, nobody understood
why I was leaving. But I like a space
that's filled up with storefronts, light poles, and cars;
I like the whoosh of a revolving door
and big screens lit up with big movie stars—
yet here I stand. And though I can ignore
Al's envy, Aunt Kate's frown, and Mama's grumbling,
I can't quite shrug off Daddy's drunken mumbling.

No, I can't shrug off Daddy's drunken mumbling
or his vague absence—not unlike my own:
he too has stepped away from all that fumbling
for happiness, his heart a well-soaked stone.
He numbs himself against frustration's ache,
but I escaped and found another world,
where color, crowds, and noise conspire to slake
all kinds of thirsts; where better booze is swirled
in fun instead of fury; where you seize
the day, it grabs back, and you feel alive;
where heat comes in the lazy, lusty wheeze
of late-night saxophones. Well, maybe I've
deserted Daddy, but there was no doubt
I had to go—I just had to get out.

I had to go; I just had to get out
of this hell-hole before I suffocated,
and that's how I feel now. Mama can pout,
Belinda Ann can push her overrated
peach pie, but I won't stay to eat a slice;
my favorite clothes won't fit if I get fat.
I don't need their approval or advice,
their false concern, the drawl of their chitchat,
their honey cut with bile. I'll take off just
as soon as I can manage it.   I'll swap
blank air for busy streets; I'll leave disgust
behind; I'll go where I can dance and shop,
where car horns blare with someone else's stress,
where I know I look fine in this red dress.

II

The Truth in Dissonance

At Symphony Hall

Don't be deceived by those of us who sit
as still as stone.   You've seen us tamely knit

our brows and fingers, but the cells inside
are madly tangled, and our dignified

façades are porous, ready to collect
the airborne gifts that gestures might deflect.

To draw and soak up every note, we seek
to be unmoving targets—open, meek—

allowing sound to breach skin easily
and then infect the blood with ecstasy.

We listen with the patience of the lame:
unmoving and unmoved are not the same.

Listening to "Dido's Lament"

(from Purcell's *Dido and Aeneas*)

We set aside our certainty that grief
would never sound quite this articulate;
we willingly suspend our disbelief
to hear strings in her heart, not from the pit.
We gladly listen to her tender plea
that we remember her but not her fate,
her noble narcissism easily
affirming things we cannot explicate.
Each repetition of the bass line brings
new tensions, though we know the story's end;
she welcomes death as she robustly sings
immortal melody. And so we bend
our brains to savor Purcell's eloquence,
discovering the truth in dissonance.

Gustav Mahler's *Kindertotenlieder*

("Songs on the Death of Children," setting poems by Friedrich Rückert)

Note: Mahler's four-year old daughter died of scarlet fever three years after he completed the song cycle.

His wife complained that he was tempting fate
by polishing poor Rückert's mournful pearls—
as if dark brilliance shouldn't fascinate
a blameless father of two healthy girls.
Still single when first tempted by the glare
of poet's grief—small gems from razor shells—
he'd married them to reedy sighs and spare
complaints wrung from the oboe, strings, and bells.
Then, wed himself, a father doubly blessed,
he set more of these lustrous words of loss
to shimmer in orchestral gold—obsessed
by beauty where the sad and splendid cross.
Meanwhile, the tide turned in a scarlet sea
that would compose his daughter's destiny.

The Pianist's Prayer

Her hands seemed to belong to someone else
as they danced through remembered rituals
and stumbled through forgotten penances.
These sometimes faithless hands,
their grace atrophied through idleness,
still moved in patterns
imprinted onto muscle by countless repetitions,
and moved her
to lean devoutly into the dissonance
and the consonance
and the cross-rhythms
and the cadences—
until, despite her lapsed pianism,
she believed
with a fervor beyond speaking in tongues:
there was singing in her fingers.

Piano Duo

for Steve

We took no vows, but we negotiate
like wife and husband: "I'll move over, dear,
if you'll make room for my low A right here."
"Of course, but after that, could you please wait
for my *rubato?*" "Sure, but don't be late
with that B-flat." "It's nice to have you near,
but how can I make my staccato clear
if you keep pedaling in measure eight?"
We cover up each other's minor slips
and share the highs and lows of married measures,
our four hands fallible, but trained and true.
With thumbs and thoughts as close as lovers' lips,
for better and for worse we practice pleasures
unknown to those who've merely said, "I do."

Gypsy Rondo

(from Haydn's Piano Trio No. 25 in G major)

Beware this effervescent little tune:
it strays and then returns repeatedly
to flirt again beneath a gypsy moon.

The pianist and the violinist soon
meet daunting tests of their dexterity
within this effervescent little tune.

The cellist's path is steadier, but strewn
with scattered notes that rise from the debris
to flirt again beneath a gypsy moon.

The other tunes, from rougher matter hewn,
back down before breeze-blown frivolity,
foiled by this effervescent little tune.

Like some frenetic helium balloon,
it flutters up, defying gravity
to flirt again beneath a gypsy moon.

Unsullied as the morning, bright as noon,
it stays up late and dances gleefully.
Beware this effervescent little tune
that flirts all night beneath a gypsy moon.

In the Alto Section

(Beethoven's Ninth Symphony)

You sit behind the orchestra, spellbound
by complex chemistry you've heard before:
a measured mix of breath and time and sound
decreed by small black icons in the score.
You recognize these runes, for you've been trained
to translate this arcane calligraphy—
to be a catalyst for unexplained
excursions into immortality.
At last you stand; at last you get to sing,
your mortal, mid-range voice admitting you
to this inspired amalgam. Finally
your notes are needed for the rendering
of gold: believe, and count, and on your cue,
supply the center of the alchemy.

Four Movements for Siblings

(after Brahms' Sextet in B-flat major, op. 18)
for Susan, Nancy, and Bill

I.   Allegro for a Middle Child
(Allegro ma non troppo)

The cellist breathes in, draws his bow, and frees
a secret kept for years by wood and string,
an alto exhalation that agrees
with high and low—a center, centering.
The undemanding middle child declines
to weep or wallow; clever and content
to be peacemaking pivot, it aligns
the others into sisterly assent.
And not the heart, exactly, but the heart
of something—something in the flesh and vein
and something in between, behind, apart
from anything that science might explain—
breathes easily at last inside of those
who live the melody the cello knows.

II.   Theme and Negotiations
(Andante, ma moderato)

A mild viola meets high-strung replies,
and so the sibling rivalry begins.
From temperate tones grow grandly strangled cries
in raucous rhythms; no one really wins.
And so they start again: they briefly heed
new rules and wrangle at a measured pace,
until contentious cellos grab the lead
and gasping violins join in the chase.
Rough strings recede, and satin threads refine
the essence of their theme: not argument
but angle, not decision but design,
not battle but unbroken filament—
a single strand that stretches with the choices
and challenges of those who raise their voices.

III. Avian Scherzo
(Scherzo: Allegro molto — Trio: Animato)

Weightlessly perched on a wing-crowded wire,
lined up to loiter, they preen and they pose:
a bevy of beaked entertainers for hire,
delicate dancers on tireless toes.
They squirm and they chirp and they fidget and natter,
friends and then foes, always feather to feather,
bickering over who's finer or fatter,
thinking of flying, forecasting the weather.
In time each takes off to take on something new—
a sycamore limb, or a worm, or a nest;
then after adventuring, hearing their cue,
they dart back to take up the dance they know best.
Lined up like suspects, but never arrested
or resting, they warble of wings newly tested.

IV. Sibling Rondo
(Poco allegretto e grazioso)

We've shared a pulse, a name, a lullaby—
and now a cello sings as if to hold
our drifting hearts together and defy
divisions, distances, and dreads untold.
Our blue eyes close in separate houses now,
our golden hair gone gray or thin, or dyed,
with different creases carved into each brow
by debts and dreams and too much to decide.
But transient defections barely strain
the old alliance; we return with ease
to games and grievances that still sustain
a gamut of familiar harmonies.
Despite well-sung goodbyes to golden days,
one tune entangles us, and blue eyes blaze.

The Real World

He taps his right foot erratically
and dips his chin from time to time,
his eyes closed
against the distractions
of flowered curtains
and solicitous name-tagged women.

Behind his crêpey eyelids
he sees the real world:
a smoky country
guarded at one border by a regiment of bottles,
at another by a sputtering neon Budweiser logo,
and ruled from a tiny stage
where he nods at Max,
who takes the next solo.

Interrupted by a kindly
but insistent mumble,
he opens his eyes
to see a frumpy stranger
who wheels him to a table
set with pink paper napkins.

This doesn't look right,
and the old lady seated to his left
smells funny,
but he plays along,
accustomed to following
someone else's lead.

And the meat loaf isn't bad.
He watches his fork
tremble its way to his mouth,
but he can still hear
the real world:
Max is on fire tonight.

Rondeau for Miss Rigby

(after Lennon and McCartney's "Eleanor Rigby")

Miss Rigby was not one to rue
her fate. No moonlit rendezvous
would make her one half of a pair,
but she had learned how not to care:
she dreamed, and gave the Lord His due.

She cleaned the church; she said a few
hellos and more Amens; she knew
that seldom did a soul ask where
Miss Rigby was.

And as she dusted sconce and pew,
her loneliness became a cue
for violins in rhythmic prayer,
although no one was really there—
and no one ever would know who
Miss Rigby was.

Rondeau for Father McKenzie

(after Lennon and McCartney's "Eleanor Rigby")

McKenzie frowns; the light is bad.
He probably should just be glad
that this decrepit rectory
is wired for electricity—
but darning socks will drive him mad.

He'd thought, when he was just a lad,
that priests found ecstasy, not sad
and clumsy-costumed piety.
McKenzie frowns

at scribbles on a yellow pad.
He'd meant to serve—a Galahad
ordained—but fears his homily
will not reach either deity
or flock. In robes of rapture clad,
McKenzie frowns.

Paul and Ringo

Do they think often of the two who've left
for loftier recording studios,
the one so good with words, the other deft
with weeping strings? No fan or tabloid knows
the whole truth of their four-way bond; no one
but Paul and Ringo really can appraise
the mania they lived— how much was fun,
how much was hell in famous yesterdays.
Do they resent it when their past persists?
The band that broke up cannot be ignored;
unbroken echoes fix its legacy.
A glaring spotlight, meant for four, insists:
each solo life is still part of a chord,
one string that vibrates with another three.

Manhattan Transfer

(Album Cover, 1975)

Four lanky tux- and gown-clad silhouettes
    flank one old-fashioned stand-up microphone;
        they arc away from its straight line, each hip
           thrust east or west in sleek sophistication,
                eight shoulders and four well-coiffed heads inclined
                back toward the mike, their sexy stance designed
           to match the half-swoon and the calculation
        that coolly blend the work of lung and lip
      in champagne-laced alliances of tone—
high style no eye or ear quickly forgets.

Livingston Taylor Live

(Pilgrim Memorial State Park, Plymouth, MA, July 2010)

As lean and blameless as a farm boy, wearing
a plain white shirt and khakis, his guitar
held close but lightly, he might just be sharing
a tale or two with old pals at a bar.
But no, he's on a stage; he sings to us,
a crowd drawn by our hunger for a fix
of laid-back Livingston. Just Liv—no fuss,
no needless noise, no pyrotechnic tricks,
just casually agile fretwork paired
with that brushed-denim voice. A bit of patter,
then songs of ease and trouble, love declared
and lost, old friends and other things that matter—
and while he sings, no blame or trouble weighs
more than the air of Carolina Days.

Ben and Annie and Us

"And so Annie waits, Annie waits, Annie waits . . ."
—Ben Folds, "Annie Waits"

Piano chords precede a single clap,
the riff repeats, our feet begin to tap,

Ben sings, and Annie waits. And waits. And waits.
For every heartache, he reiterates

that word. The story ought to make us blue,
especially when we learn that he, too,

has waited, and the song abruptly ends,
along with hope for these two lonely friends.

She's waited "for the last time"—so he sings—
as cars pass by and her phone never rings.

But we can't summon up too much distress;
we're taken by the lilt of loneliness.

In fact, we may just make them wait again—
just press a button, so that we hear Ben

repeat it all. Ben probably won't mind,
but Annie might consider us unkind,

for Ben reminds us that "it's getting late"—
and yet we love to listen to her wait.

The Playlist of the Woeful Middle-Aged Man

Old pop songs pandering to his regrets
renew the failures of old fantasies,
recalling woes a wiser man forgets.

Dan Fogelberg or Billy Joel upsets
his mid-life calm; he weeps at minor keys
in old songs pandering to his regrets.

He's "Blue" with Joni Mitchell, JT sets
him off with "Lonesome Road," and each reprise
recalls the woes a wiser man forgets.

As Crosby, Stills, and Nash croon on cassettes,
he's "Helplessly Hoping," brought to his knees
by pop songs pandering to his regrets.

Although catharsis never comes, he lets
his iPod replay Carly's elegies,
and dwells on woes a wiser man forgets.

He sighs with Harry Chapin, and he frets
to Bonnie Raitt's raw-silk soliloquies—
old pop songs pandering to his regrets,
recalling woes a wiser man forgets.

III

A Year in New England

January

Is this the ballyhooed beginning cheered
by thousands in Times Square? The favored time
for making resolutions real, the prime
redemptive chance all hailed as midnight neared?
An icebound analyst would give the edge
to pessimists, who know what winter weighs.
With frozen fortitude, can we still raise
a glass to make another New Year's pledge?
Unfazed, the phoenix rises every year
from ash of Auld Lang Syne into a cold
refrain that goads the spirit into growth.
And January's dare provokes no fear
in those who toast the future—for they hold
cups full of faith, or foolishness, or both.

Winter Boats

Becalmed in back yards, cold and mortified,
boats hold their breath until the day when stiff
blue tarps can be removed, when bows can glide
across blue bays. For months, the sleekest skiff
looks clumsy, inconvenienced by its own
unfloated weight, bound to a rusty trailer,
as buoyant as an old shoe or a stone,
when she should be bound only to a sailor.
But he's a summer creature too: he knows
how briefly hulls and hearts are light, how short
the breathing season is. It's he who tows
her, come the fall, to this ignoble port
beside the shed; he leaves her high and dry
and heavy with a longing for July.

Winter Confrontations

Weightless, colorless,
soundless flakes somehow subdue
a sturdy gray oak.

The depth of the white,
half-frozen mantle exceeds
the height of your boot.

The huge-handed clutch
of steely cold penetrates
your parka's embrace.

The sun only glares—
until it meets its eager
match in your child's eyes.

Boston Common at Twilight

(after the painting by Childe Hassam)

What winter twilight hasn't quite erased
directs the eye, with brown geometry,
to one small girl bent slightly from the waist.

The straight line of the city street is traced
by paragons of verticality
that winter twilight hasn't quite erased:

row houses, trolleys, trees. All stiffly braced
against the dark, they frame, protectively,
a small girl bending slightly from the waist.

A lady in long skirts, tall and thin-faced,
extends her left hand, prompting us to see
what winter twilight hasn't quite erased,

what icy days and nights have not yet chased
away: a few birds, waiting hopefully
before a small girl who bends from the waist

to feed them. Snow-white cold has been displaced
by sepia-toned small-scale charity
that winter twilight hasn't quite erased:
one small girl bending slightly from the waist.

Snowmelt

The melting snow engenders mud
or flood

or both. It nurtures dormant roots,
new shoots,

and nascent hope: its dirty streams
feed dreams.

The Optimism of New England Peepers

For Maxine

Our woods harbor amphibious clairvoyants,
shorter than a thumb
and lighter than a quarter,
who will signal us
with "peeping"
when the worst is over.

These tiny frogs
pick a morning in late March
to serenade us
with a sound like tiny sleigh bells—
cold Christmas ringing
in their improbable proclamation
of spring.

We want to believe them;
their evolutionary credentials
should trump our continuing need
for the electric blanket.

We'd like to join their chorus,
but our faith is weak;
we've seen snow in April.

The Lilac

The tiny lilac buds just barely bloom:
they affably unwink their pastel eyes
at brasher blossoms, emanating sighs
of self-assured but delicate perfume.
Reliable, requiring little care,
companionably clustered lilac flowers
attest to understatement's heady powers,
as neatly gathered nuance fills the air.
And while the compact purple clouds expand
and multiply, their swoon-inducing scent
persuades a jaded world that it was meant
to bow before brief beauty's mute command.
The lilac's life of small perfections poses
a challenge rarely met by men or roses.

Yard Sale Pros

They swarm the cluttered lawn by ten of eight,
inspecting dog-eared books, scarred maple hutches,
worn skis, a chipped but cheerful Christmas plate—
no tattered treasure will escape their clutches.

The grey-haired lady in the lime green slacks
peers past the hockey sticks and rusty bikes,
beyond the Hummels and homemade knickknacks,
and then, triumphant, spots a lamp she likes.

Above its sturdy base of tarnished brass,
its ecru linen shade is trimmed with beads
that dangle like hard tears of cloudy glass—
a piece of lustrous loot amid the weeds.

The price tag says ten dollars—what a steal!—
but still she haggles (why not save a buck?),
and pays just five. Delighted with the deal,
she grins and totes her prize out to the truck.

And there sits Ralph, her patient, portly prince,
and bless his heart, he grins right back at her.
He hates the lamp, but doesn't even wince;
he's always an agreeable chauffeur.

He doesn't care how many times they stop;
he'll wait, and listen to sports radio.
He loves the Red Sox, and she loves to shop—
a happy pair, each one a yard sale pro.

To the Ocean in Summer

The barely dressed now come to worship you:
ungainly flesh squeezed into scraps of red,
hot pink, and purple speckling your cool blue
like live confetti grossly overfed.
The riotous, unruly bodies flail
against your flawless choreography
of air and water, and their voices wail
as if to join your song, but out of key.
Their adoration seasonal but real,
the spandex-clad and bulging-bellied masses
attend upon you with immodest zeal
until the fevered tryst of summer passes.
And you indulge the self-indulgent crowd,
your dazzle and your dignity unbowed.

Tide and Terrain

(Long Beach, Plymouth, MA)

I didn't know that it would be high tide;
I never check the charts. I felt the need
for salt air and drove east to walk a wide
soft swath of gold dust—but twice-daily greed
for territory had provoked the bay
to occupy the shore right to the rocks,
the beach now intermittent, and my way
a mix of grainy mud and granite blocks.
Compelled by this terrain to improvise,
I strolled through water, then on well-soaked sand,
then on the jetty. When the shoreline sifted
itself, I did the same, my feet and eyes
adjusting as each moment made its stand
against the last, then drowned as power shifted.

Gloucester Harbor

(after the painting by Winslow Homer)

To know such calm as this—a bay
just barely undulant, a day
that starts to hail its own demise
with indigo and coral skies,
a friend to share your boat—you may

need only to observe it: pay
attention to such gifts and lay
aside the worries of the wise.
To know such calm,

you need not know this waterway,
or feel this floating hammock sway,
or wield an oar. Just train your eyes
on painted peace, and exercise
your slightly aged naïveté
to know such calm.

Newport Mansions, Observed from the Cliff Walk

(Newport, Rhode Island)

I don't want to admire this opulence:
I want to frown on these icons of greed,
rejecting this seaside extravagance.

But maybe if I didn't count my cents
and dollars just to meet each daily need,
I'd readily admire this opulence.

The chandeliers might not cause such offense
if gas bills didn't make my budget bleed
and new shoes weren't an extravagance.

Within these marble walls, behind immense
arched windows, there once lived a moneyed breed
that knew no want. Admiring opulence

like this, while some folks live in cars or tents,
just seems unseemly. We could house and feed
so many with half this extravagance.

I walk along the sea—at no expense—
past Vanderbilt back yards. I will concede
that yes, I do admire this opulence,
but I prefer the sea's extravagance.

August

The downward slope of summer modulates
the angle of our pleasures as it trains
reluctant eyes upon the lower plains,
where imminent nostalgia coolly waits.
Still coddled by a kind and lofty light,
we toast the sunset earlier each day,
like open-faced sunflowers that betray
a naïve over-ripeness in their height.
We're past peak season for the kind of heat
that met with merciless humidity
in waves that drained our bodies and the land—
but this deliverance is bittersweet:
we clutch our sweating glasses of iced tea
as tightly as we'd grasp a mother's hand.

Remnant

Well past the hurricane's last gasp, a week
beyond the need for candles, several days
past panicking about our swollen creek,
and after sweating through the cleanup phase,
we put away the rakes and power saws
and hailed the resurrection of our phones;
at peace again with nature's random laws,
we'd lost the terror blown into our bones.
But one branch still sprawled in our neighbor's yard:
a gawky, wind-lopped limb some eight feet long,
leaves brown and shriveling—a calling card
left by the storm, a scrap of something strong.
It questioned, in its battered dignity,
our definition of recovery.

Mute Migrants

No seasonal honk
        alerted me,
            no flapping of wings,
                only an impulse
                    to look up and appraise
                        this morning's edition
                                    of sky.
                        And there they flew,
                in the rough draft of a V—
                not the most precise parade,
                but swift as a regatta
        and sure of their southward course,
        silently signaling their itinerary
        in dark splotches
    of disappearing
ink.

In Autumn's Rust

"The rusty autumn gold is glorious."
—John Updike, "Endpoint"

In autumn's rust, maturity
meets wear and tear, and victory
proclaims that races have their ends.
The planet tilts, the prism bends,
and gold soon bows to gravity.

But with the chill of irony,
despite decay, the currency
of stamina yields dividends
 in autumn's rust.

The self's new crust of fluency
succeeds the garbled vanity
of summer; glory wisely spends
its coin, makes love and makes amends.
We meet our virtuosity
in autumn's rust.

November Rose

An unexpected legacy, this rose
will prick the heart more sharply than its thorn
impales the skin. In autumn's grip, it grows
to such unlikely splendor that we mourn
the days it should have seen—that succulent
mid-summer spell of sun-ripe reveries—
and we distrust its claim of insolent
good health amid stripped skeletons of trees.
Ingenuous denial feeds its pink,
persistent life—but our sophistication
ensures a bitter flavor as we drink
its beauty like a funeral libation.
July's bequest blooms on, defiantly:
a misplaced emblem of vitality.

December

Arriving modestly, without a sound,
the first snow of the season fills the night
with tiny flakes of other-worldly light
that settles in pale patches on the ground.
The stone-cold air turns flannel-soft, transformed
by small wet stars that fall and thereby lift
the eye and heart—a fragile, frozen gift
that leaves our spirits fortified and warmed.
Another silent night may come to mind,
another star, another gift, but He
need not be sought as heaven falls to earth
in icy, cloud-spun pieces that will find
the pious and the pagan, equally
anointing all who see the season's birth.

IV

Bliss

Sometime after the Golden Anniversary

For decades, nothing fazed them. Nothing etched
a lasting scar into the single skin
through which both breathed, a skin that stretched
to cope with kids, careers, and crises—thin
enough to take in every pleasure, thick
enough to outlast loss and anger, taut
enough to hold when one or both were sick,
and slack enough for comfort—so they thought.
But what the decades finally did appalled
their children and their friends: it seemed that age
could lacerate what nothing else defaced.
In unfamiliar pain, they cruelly called
each other names, applied no salve but rage,
and tore away what no graft could replace.

They tore away what no graft could replace,
their bond obliterated by a shared
abhorrence of how wrinkles mar a face
and how the years leave hips and eyes impaired.
It should have brought them closer: an occasion
for empathy, a source of anecdotes
they'd tell in tandem, proving their equation
still added up, could still inspire odes
to love. But facing time's unkindness, they
unkindly poked and cut until the harm
was past repair, their single rampart shredded.
And what they bloodied, what they scratched away,
was the protection of a loving arm
against a foe that they had never dreaded.

Against a foe that they had never dreaded,
they must have sensed they'd lose—and so they fought
each other. Cells and muscle once embedded
beneath a single skin split open, caught
on barbs of tarnished gold. It was a shock
to all who knew them and had long believed
this pair unbreakable. How could the clock
and calendar leave so much to be grieved?
Observers of their mutual injury
lamented, gossiped, guessed at who had wronged
the other more. And yet, despite all this,
no one recanted years of jealousy:
without exception, other couples longed
to share one skin like theirs, and know their bliss.

Subtext for Sam

Dear Sam *(more dear to me than I should say—*
in fact, I'll highlight "Dear" and press "Delete"),
Your newsy e-mail brightened up my day.
(My heart is pounding!—but I'll be discreet.)
I'm glad to hear you got that raise at last
(your worth cannot be measured in mere gold!),
and sorry that your Aunt Lou-Ann has passed
(but I could comfort you with charms untold).
And yes, the market forecasts have been frightful
(who cares for wealth if we can't be together?),
and yes, these autumn days have been delightful
(I hate this chattering about the weather!).
Let's keep in touch, my *(dear, illicit)* friend.
(I leave out "Love" and sigh as I hit "Send.")

Pantoum for a Disappearing Pair

She whispers, "I need to get out of here."
He smiles at last. Their wishes coincide,
and both of them know how to disappear
before short tempers and tall drinks collide.

He smiles. At last, their wishes coincide,
while lately their agreements have been rare.
Before short tempers and tall drinks collide,
they'll find a back door and get out of there.

Though lately their agreements have been rare,
they both dislike lame jokes and cut-rate gin.
They find a back door and get out of there,
abandoning the unconvincing din.

They both dislike lame jokes and cut-rate gin
and parties where the past still tends the bar.
Abandoning the unconvincing din,
he relishes the silence in their car.

At parties where the past still tends the bar,
the same old small talk seldom drowns out dread.
He relishes the silence in their car;
soon they'll be home, curled up in their warm bed.

The same old small talk seldom drowns out dread,
but both of them know how to disappear.
Soon they're at home. Curled up in their warm bed,
she whispers, "I need to get out of here."

Another Plaster Idol Smashed to Bits

You didn't think, this time, that you'd expected
too much, that you had set him up for blame
right from the start, your high hopes misdirected,
until the very moment he became
another plaster idol smashed to bits.
Of course, you never know until the smashing
that something's made of plaster. Oddly, it's
surprising every time—the silent crashing
an insult to the heart's ear. But you'd swear
that this time had been different: you had taken
this man for mortal, hadn't made him wear
a halo or a laurel wreath. You're shaken
to hear again the din of mute disaster,
to breathe again this dust that tastes of plaster.

At Last

She'd all but given up. The odds were long,
she knew; she was more likely to be struck
by lightning. Yes, her eyes could use a tuck,
her hair was graying—but her voice was strong,
and with a bit of pride she sang her song
of middle age: she didn't dye or pluck
or mourn the doors now long since closed. Her luck
at least had kept her safe from Mr. Wrong.
She seldom gave a thought to Mr. Right
these days—although she kept on trying doors,
the way a watchman on the late shift does,
more dutiful than curious, and slight-
ly weary. She met cads and oafs and bores,
then opened one more door—and there he was.

Love and Shoes

"You show up on your first date with your best shoes on,
hoping to get to a place where you keep your shoes off."
—Elizabeth Berg, *Once Upon a Time There Was You*

Too old for yet another foolish crush,
she does admit to savoring this sweet,
disorienting, and delicious rush:
he strolls in, and she's lighter on her feet.
She used to wedge her feet into high heels,
as if to lift romance to breathless heights,
each pointy toe an arrow toward ideals
of true love and away from lonely nights.
By now, though, shoes have taken quite a toll
on both her budget and her straining arches;
this man will have to like a flat, scuffed sole
or barefoot walks, instead of style's forced marches.
If he likes her in flip-flops—maybe less—
then they might stride right into happiness.

Pas de Deux

for RTK & MLK

Their dance defined by melodies few know,
they move with matchless grace, and deftly hide
the wear of well-lived decades as they glide
in happy synchrony learned long ago.
Their lithe duet has not eluded pain—
but when they meet despair's discordant tone,
they dip and sway, resilience having grown
through years of heeding one sublime refrain.
For neither cadences of loss and fear
nor common time has ever stilled their feet;
uncommon hearts discern a subtler beat
and live the music others hardly hear.
In compromise as well as celebration,
their two-step traces love's collaboration.

About the Author

Jean L. Kreiling is a Professor of Music at Bridgewater State University in Massachusetts; she previously taught English at Western Carolina University in North Carolina. Kreiling's poems have appeared widely in print and online journals, including *American Arts Quarterly, Angle, The Evansville Review, Measure,* and *Mezzo Cammin,* as well as in several anthologies. She is a past winner of the *String Poet* Prize and the *Able Muse* Write Prize for Poetry; she has been a finalist for the Richard Wilbur Poetry Award, the Howard Nemerov Sonnet Award, the Frost Farm Prize, and the *Dogwood* Poetry Prize.